THE
ONE-MINUT
HAPPINESS
JOURNAL

365 WAYS TO CAPTURE THE JOY
IN YOUR LIFE EVERY DAY

EVA OLSEN

CASTLE POINT BOOKS
NEW YORK

ISBN 978-1-250-23477-3 (trade paperback)

Design by Domino Design

Images used under license from Shutterstock.com

Our books may be purchased in bulk for promotional, educational, or business use. Please
contact your local bookseller or the Macmillan Corporate and Premium Sales Department at
1-800-221-7945, extension 5442, or by email at MacmillanSpecialMarkets@macmillan.com.

First Edition: October 2019

10 9 8 7 6 5 4 3 2 1

THIS JOURNAL BELONGS TO:

_____

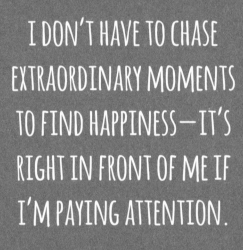

I DON'T HAVE TO CHASE EXTRAORDINARY MOMENTS TO FIND HAPPINESS—IT'S RIGHT IN FRONT OF ME IF I'M PAYING ATTENTION.

—Brené Brown

INTRODUCTION

WE'RE ALL SEARCHING FOR MORE JOY IN OUR LIVES.
The good news: happiness is surprisingly easy to find without undergoing a complete life overhaul. What's the secret? Just take a step back for a moment, look around you, and take it all in. You can focus on all the good in your life in just one minute a day, with the help of this book!

The 365 prompts on the pages that follow are designed to be simple, enjoyable ways to appreciate the happiness already present and embrace available opportunities for expanded joy. Make the pocket of time you spend each day with *The One-Minute Happiness Journal* a gift to yourself!

WRITE DOWN A SONG LYRIC (in fun lettering, if you like) that's guaranteed to make you smile whenever you hear it. **BONUS:** Make that song a ringtone.

_____

_____

_____

_____

_____

RECALL ONE ACT OF KINDNESS you experienced or witnessed today.

_____

_____

_____

_____

_____

_____

FIND THE MOST BEAUTIFUL SIGHT in whatever space you're in right now. Draw it here.

THINK OF THE AFFECTIONATE NICKNAMES friends and family call you. Jot them down.

GO TO THE FIRST PHOTO on your phone's camera roll, then write a caption for it.

_____

_____

_____

_____

_____

_____

BRING TO MIND THE BEST GIFT you ever received—and what made it so special. Write about it or sketch it below. **BONUS:** Pull it out and hold it if it's tangible and you still have it.

STEP OUTSIDE, TAKE A BREATH, and list five things you are grateful for in this moment.

1. _____

2. _____

3. _____

4. _____

5. _____

SEND AN ENCOURAGING TEXT to someone special in your life. How did the act make you feel?

_____

_____

_____

_____

_____

_____

_____

CHOOSE ONE CHILDLIKE THING YOU CAN DO in the next 24 hours. (Examples: Eat ice cream for breakfast or look for hidden objects in the clouds.) Write it down, then do it! **BONUS:** Come back to this entry later and record what emotions the activity evoked.

SIMPLY SMILE—even if you need to fake it! Research shows the activation of facial muscles associated with smiling triggers a very real mood boost in the brain. Draw your face as a smiley face for inspiration.

ATTACH A PHOTO OF, OR DRAW, A PLACE that brings you happiness—it could be a faraway exotic beach, a mountaintop, a campfire circled with family and friends, or a simple hammock in your own backyard. Try to picture being there whenever you need a boost.

PLAN TO ATTEND AT LEAST ONE TICKETED EVENT in the next few weeks. Jot down some event ideas to seek out and any companions you'll invite on the ticket stub below. Even the anticipation will bring you joy.

TAKE A SELFIE with the craziest filter you can find. Then feel free to laugh at yourself. **BONUS:** Send it to a close friend and ask for a caption. Record the response.

THINK OF ONE THING that someone close to you has asked to borrow many times. Make a pledge to give the item to that person for keeps.

_____

_____

_____

_____

_____

BRING IN A TOUCH OF THE OUTDOORS—fresh flowers, pine cones, a fallen branch, shells, stones, or a found feather. Sketch or write about what you chose below.

RECORD THREE SMALL VICTORIES from your day. They could be as simple as returning a phone call or drinking more than one glass of water.

1. _____
_____

2. _____
_____

3. _____
_____

ORGANIZE WHAT YOU ARE GOING TO WEAR tomorrow in words or pictures below. When you look good, you feel good.

REMOVE A FEW APPS from your phone. What mobile (and mental) clutter did you realize you can live better without?

⊗ _____
⊗ _____
⊗ _____
⊗ _____
⊗ _____
⊗ _____
⊗ _____

CALL A LOVED ONE AND PLAY 30 seconds of a special song. What was the song and what was the person's reaction?

_____
_____
_____
_____
_____
_____
_____

PRESERVE WORDS OF WISDOM —whether they come from a famous author or a family member—that hold special meaning for you.

"

,,

ATTACH A PHOTO OF, OR DRAW, A SMILE that means the world to you.

ATTACH A PHOTO OF, OR DRAW, A MOMENT that filled you with pride.

TREAT YOURSELF TO SOMETHING FRESH —maybe flowers, fruit, a notebook, or a start. What did you choose, and how it did make you feel?

_____

_____

_____

_____

_____

_____

_____

RECORD THE BEST THING YOU HEARD all day—whether it was a baby's laugh or a great song you haven't heard in ages.

_____

_____

_____

_____

_____

_____

_____

RELEASE YOURSELF FROM SOMETHING in your surroundings that drains your energy and joy. Maybe it's an unfinished project or an object that holds unpleasant memories. No explanation needed—commit it to the trash can below, then get rid of it in real life as well!

_____

_____

_____

_____

_____

BELIEVE IN MAGIC. At 11:11 (a.m. or p.m.), make a wish and record it here.

LIST FIVE TREASURES IN YOUR LIFE. While possessions aren't everything, certain objects can bring comfort and joy—even if just by association with memories.

1. _____

2. _____

3. _____

4. _____

5. _____

DESCRIBE A FAVORITE PHOTO that you've taken. **BONUS:** Attach a copy of it below.

DESCRIBE A FAVORITE PHOTO that has been taken of you. **BONUS:** Attach a copy of it below.

RECALL IN WORDS OR PICTURES one of the best ways you have ever spent money on yourself.

RECALL IN WORDS OR PICTURES one of the best ways you have ever spent money on someone else.

FILL IN THE BLANK with as many answers as come to mind: *I can't contain my laughter when _____.*

_____   _____

_____   _____

_____   _____

_____   _____

_____   _____

_____   _____

LIST A FEW THINGS in your life that are messy but still beautiful.

_____   _____

_____   _____

_____   _____

_____   _____

_____   _____

_____   _____

DRAW A T-SHIRT THAT MAKES YOU SMILE, whether it's one you currently own or one you dream up.

DESCRIBE IN DETAIL THE LAST GREAT HUG you received.

GET OUT A CALENDAR and pick a day to make yours. What day did you choose, and what will you do?

_____

_____

_____

_____

_____

_____

WRITE THE TITLES of some of the best books you've ever read on the spines below.

RECALL THE BEST PACKAGE you've ever received in the mail.

_____
_____
_____
_____
_____
_____
_____

FIND THE BEST TEXT you've received in the past week. What did it say?

_____
_____
_____
_____
_____
_____

DESCRIBE YOUR FAVORITE WAY TO WAKE UP. Can you make this happen more often?

_____

_____

_____

_____

LIST SEVEN THINGS THAT ARE A BEAUTIFUL FIT —from clothing to people in your life.

1. _____

2. _____

3. _____

4. _____

5. _____

6. _____

7. _____

THINK OF THE LAST PERSON YOU MADE SMILE. Who was it, and how did you do it?

_____

_____

_____

_____

_____

_____

CAPTURE THE WORDS YOUR FRIENDS AND FAMILY would use to describe you and why they like spending time with you.

_____   _____

_____   _____

_____   _____

_____   _____

_____   _____

LOOK AT YOUR LIFE THROUGH A DOG'S EYES. What simple care and comforts do you have to be grateful for?

BRING TO MIND A PERSON IN YOUR LIFE who stands with you through it all. What specific traits do you appreciate in that loved one?

DESCRIBE A TRADITION IN YOUR LIFE that brings you joy.

_____

_____

_____

_____

_____

_____

READ ONE PAGE from a sacred text or source of inspiration. What words from your reading inspire you?

_____

_____

_____

_____

_____

_____

RECORD THE OFTEN UNDERAPPRECIATED THINGS that worked well for you today—from perfectly toasted bread to a car that started.

_____   _____

_____   _____

_____   _____

_____   _____

_____   _____

FILL IN THE BLANK with as many answers as come to mind: _I love my_ _____.

_____   _____

_____   _____

_____   _____

_____   _____

_____   _____

CREATE QUICK FREE SPACE somewhere in your life—clear off a counter of clutter or mark a weekend on your calendar "no commitments." Record your step taken, then breathe.

_____

_____

_____

_____

_____

LEARN A JOKE. It can be decently good or so bad it makes others groan. Record it here, along with whom you plan to tell it to.

_____

_____

_____

_____

_____

_____

LEAVE AN ANONYMOUS STICKY NOTE to let someone know that you appreciate something they did for you or someone else, or that you just appreciate the kind of person they are. Record what you share below.

_____

_____

_____

_____

_____

GO AHEAD AND USE IT! Whether it's a Champagne glass for your morning orange juice or fancy jewelry on a Wednesday, jot down what special-occasion saves you can break out to simply celebrate *today*.

_____

_____

_____

_____

_____

CONGRATULATE YOURSELF FOR THE BEST THING you make in the kitchen—whether it's a chocolate soufflé or a simple cup of coffee. BONUS: Treat a friend to this specialty.

CREATE A LINEUP of the super-heroes in your life with pictures and captions.

SKETCH OR DESCRIBE THE ONE PIECE of clothing that makes you feel most comfortable. Judge only by how it makes you feel, not how it looks. **BONUS:** Wear it as you write.

INVENT A SECRET GREETING with a loved one. Is it something you do or say (or both) to share a special sentiment just between the two of you?

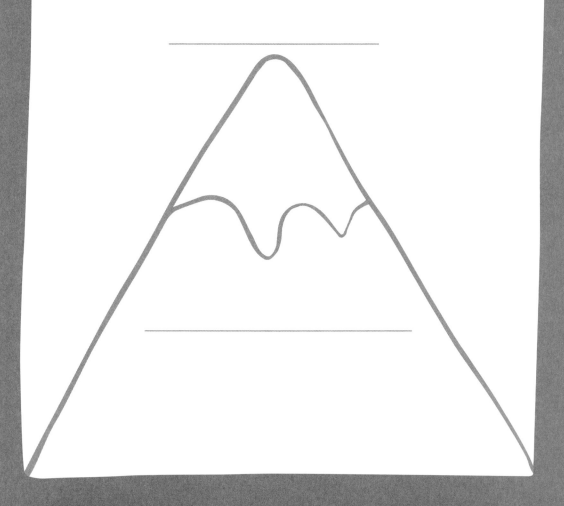

BRIGHTEN YOUR DAY by choosing to write in a color other than blue, black, or graphite. Doodle in your chosen color(s) below.

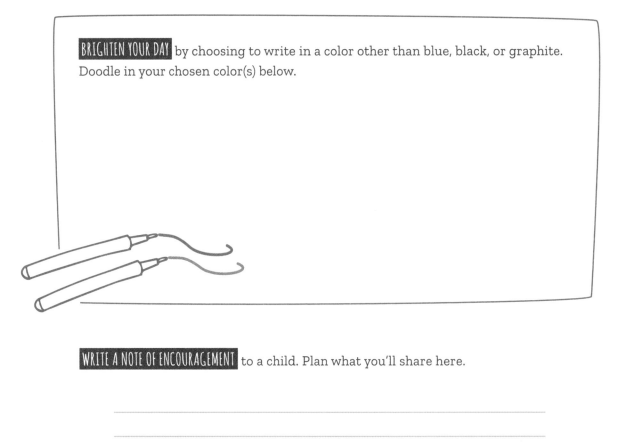

WRITE A NOTE OF ENCOURAGEMENT to a child. Plan what you'll share here.

in your life who will always answer when you text or call.

THINK ABOUT THE BEST NIGHTS OF SLEEP you've ever had. What factors contributed, and how can you include them in your nighttime routine more often?

RECALL THE MOST FUN VEHICLE you've ever driven or ridden in. Draw yourself in it below.

CAPTURE THE SOUNDTRACK OF HOME. What sounds bring you happiness with their familiarity?

THINK OF YOUR FAVORITE SIMPLE PLEASURE to shop for—say, at a price point less than $10. Recall your last shopping trip or plan your next shopping trip for this item.

_____

_____

_____

_____

_____

_____

INVENT A WORD that encompasses the crazy joy in your life. Write it in fun lettering below; use it often.

BEAUTIFY YOUR COMPUTER DESKTOP. Take care of those floating files, then set a gorgeous scene as your wallpaper. What scene did you choose?

_____
_____
_____
_____
_____
_____

REMEMBER A BOOK YOU LOVED AS CHILD in words or pictures.
BONUS: Send it as an anonymous donation to a school or childcare center.

START A BACK-AND-FORTH ELECTRONIC GAME with a friend—whether it's chess or a word game—as a reminder to check in with each other regularly. Limit it to one move or turn each day. Whom will you invite, and what will you play?

GO BAREFOOT SOMEWHERE THAT FEELS GREAT. Did you treat your feet to sand, soft grass, a fountain, a fuzzy rug, or another texture?

WRITE A THANK-YOU NOTE to a teacher who made a difference in your life. Plan what you'll share here.

_____
_____
_____
_____
_____
_____

COLOR AND NAME THE PAINT HUE that fits your happy mood.

ENVISION THE BODY OF WATER

that makes you happiest—whether it's the ocean on a wild surf day; a remote, serene lake; a hot tub at the gym or spa; or your very own bathtub. Capture where it is and how it makes you feel.

_____

_____

_____

_____

_____

GRAB AN EMPTY CONTAINER that will now be a gratitude jar you can add to each day. Make your first contribution and record it here.

_____

_____

_____

_____

TAKE A JOY WALK. At some point in your day, wander inside or outside with no real purpose in mind. What did you see along the way?

_____

_____

_____

_____

_____

_____

THINK OF A TIME YOU FELT LIKE EVERYTHING WAS RIGHT IN THE WORLD. Where were you and what were you doing?

_____

_____

_____

_____

_____

_____

_____

LOOK UP THE DATE of the next full moon, and plan to get outside and bask in the glow (weather permitting) that night. When and where will you take in the moonlight?

DESCRIBE A FAVORITE FEATURE of, or a special item in, your bedroom.

APPRECIATE SOMETHING that *didn't* happen during your day.

_____

_____

_____

_____

_____

_____

SHARE ANY NAMES you have for inanimate objects in your life. (It adds everyday play!)

_____   _____

_____   _____

_____   _____

_____   _____

_____   _____

CREATE A FALL BUCKET LIST of activities you want to do before the season ends this year.

_____   _____
_____   _____
_____   _____
_____   _____
_____   _____
_____   _____

GIVE THANKS FOR THE BEST INVITATION you ever received.

_____
_____
_____
_____
_____
_____
_____
_____

MAKE YOUR BED. As you straighten the covers, recognize how you've made progress toward smoothing over one rough area of your life.

_____

_____

_____

_____

_____

SELECT ONE SPECIAL PHOTO that's been trapped on your phone or computer. Make a move to print two physical copies—one to paste here, one to display somewhere you'll see it every day.

DREAM UP YOUR PERFECT BREAKFAST in words or pictures. Then make it or order it one day this week.

LIST FIVE PEOPLE WHO MAKE YOU HAPPY. **BONUS:** Reach out to one of them through a quick call or text.

1. _____

2. _____

3. _____

4. _____

5. _____

BLOW OUT STRESS by blowing soap bubbles or bubblegum bubbles. Or simply let out a big exhale through your mouth. What worries do you envision blowing out?

THINK OF THE BEST THING YOU HELD today and how it felt.

DESCRIBE IN WORDS OR PICTURES

the last experience that moved you to tears of joy.

DESCRIBE IN WORDS OR PICTURES

the last experience that made you giggle uncontrollably.

CAPTURE YOUR EARLIEST HAPPY MEMORY. Try to include all the sensory details you can remember.

_____

_____

_____

_____

_____

GRAB YOUR FAVORITE BALL. Toss it high in the air or throw it as far as you can. What did you select, and how far did it go?

_____

_____

_____

_____

_____

DESCRIBE THE BEST HOMEMADE GIFT you've ever received.

_____

_____

_____

_____

_____

_____

DESCRIBE THE BEST HOMEMADE GIFT you've ever given.

_____

_____

_____

_____

_____

_____

RECALL A TIME WHEN YOU WERE EXCITED TO VOTE —whether it was for a presidential candidate or the destination of the family vacation.

_____

_____

_____

_____

_____

_____

DRAW YOUR FAVORITE WAY to spend alone time.

WRITE AN ENCOURAGING MESSAGE or verse in a pretty card and leave it where a complete stranger will randomly find it. How did it feel?

_____

_____

_____

_____

_____

CREATE THE FORECAST for your perfect weather day.

MAKE A WISH UPON A STAR. Record it here.

SHARE HOW YOU CELEBRATE your favorite holiday—in words or pictures or both.

CONSIDER WHERE AND HOW unexpected joy popped up today.

MAKE IT A GAME TO GET OUTSIDE as many times as you can today—even if for just a minute at a time. Come back and record how you feel afterward.

LIST YOUR FIVE FAVORITE things to do with your family.

1. _____
2. _____
3. _____
4. _____
5. _____

LIST YOUR FIVE FAVORITE things to do with your friends.

1. _____
2. _____
3. _____
4. _____
5. _____

CREATE YOUR PERFECT TACO below. Soft or hard shell? What goes inside? Mild or spicy? **BONUS:** Put it on the menu for a lunch or dinner this week.

REMEMBER A TIME WHEN YOUR UNIQUE TALENTS were able to help someone.

LIST FIVE ANIMALS THAT MAKE YOU HAPPY —whether they're pets you have or know, characters in books or movies, or social media stars.

1. _____

2. _____

3. _____

4. _____

5. _____

SHARE A GOOD WORD and smile with someone who serves you today. What was the reaction?

_____

_____

_____

_____

_____

_____

_____

RECORD SOMETHING NEW you learned today—no matter how small it may seem.

_____

_____

_____

_____

_____

GIVE THANKS FOR SOMETHING OLD you own that brings you happiness.

_____

_____

_____

_____

_____

THINK BACK TO THE BEST FIREWORKS display you've ever seen. Where were you? What was the occasion?

_____

_____

_____

_____

_____

_____

PINPOINT A MOMENT WHEN YOUR SENSES were awakened and you felt abundantly alive today.

_____

_____

_____

_____

_____

_____

_____

LISTEN TO ONE BIRDCALL with the help of an app or web search. As you listen, sketch the bird you've chosen or write a few interesting facts about it.

CHOOSE A BIRTHDAY that stands out in your memory. What made it special?
BONUS: Find a photo from the celebration.

DESCRIBE A PIECE OF ART that stirs your soul and how you discovered it.

CONSIDER WHAT HAS BEEN THE MOST MEANINGFUL KISS of your life—whether deeply passionate or familiar and sentimental.

DRAW A MEANINGFUL TATTOO you either have or might consider getting one day—even if it's just temporary.

RECALL A TIME WHEN YOU SPOTTED A RAINBOW. **BONUS:** Post or draw a picture.

FEED AN ANIMAL —whether it's your pet, ducks at the park, or birds in the backyard. Record the experience.

_____

_____

_____

_____

_____

_____

SUMMARIZE THE BEST PART of your day as if writing a movie review.

_____

_____

_____

_____

_____

GO TO YOUR FAVORITE SPOT in your home. Come up with three words that capture what you love about this place.

1. _____

2. _____

3. _____

DESCRIBE A DREAM TRIP you would like to take someday. Even if the travel possibility is far off, research shows that anticipation can spike happiness.

_____

_____

_____

_____

_____

_____

_____

WRITE A FEW LINES OF A POEM that brings you joy. The words may come from a favorite poet or your own heart.

APPRECIATE WHAT AROMA coming from the oven always warms your heart.

CELEBRATE A SHOW OF CONFIDENCE someone gave you this week.

LOOK OUT A WINDOW and draw something that catches your eye.

WHISTLE A SILLY SONG you remember from childhood. What did you choose, and how did it make you feel?

CHOOSE ONE FRIEND whom you interact with more on social media than in real life. What three things do you appreciate most about your friendship?
BONUS: Send him or her a message of appreciation for support from afar.

CELEBRATE 10 THINGS THAT ARE WEIRD but wonderful about you and your life.

1. _____
2. _____
3. _____
4. _____
5. _____
6. _____
7. _____
8. _____
9. _____
10. _____

DRAW WHAT BRINGS YOU THE MOST JOY at an amusement park—a certain ride, a food treat, or just spending time with others.

FILL IN THE BLANK with as many answers as come to mind: *I am a strong* _____.

1. _____
2. _____
3. _____
4. _____
5. _____
6. _____
7. _____
8. _____
9. _____
10. _____

1. _____
2. _____
3. _____
4. _____
5. _____
6. _____
7. _____
8. _____
9. _____
10. _____

PLAY A MUSICAL INSTRUMENT. No actual instruments on hand? Play anything that will make a noise—move wind chimes, pair spoons and glasses, drum with a pencil, or shake a canister. How did it feel?

_____

_____

_____

_____

_____

CAPTURE THE BEST ADVICE you ever received and the wise counselor who gave it.

_____

_____

_____

_____

_____

_____

_____

SCAN YOUR COMMUNITY NEWS to find a headline full of hope.
Write it or paste it here.

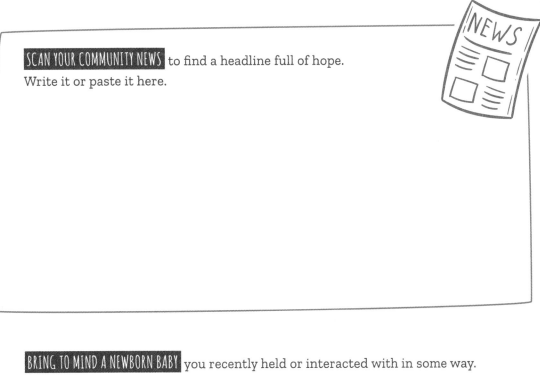

BRING TO MIND A NEWBORN BABY you recently held or interacted with in some way.
Who was it, and how did it make you feel?

REVEAL ONE GUILTY PLEASURE. Then drop the guilt.

_____

_____

_____

_____

_____

LOOK UP A TOY you loved from your childhood. Is it still being produced? If so, how has it changed? How has it stayed the same? Bonus: Give this toy as a gift to a child in your life.

_____

_____

_____

_____

_____

DESCRIBE ONE TASK that most people would consider work but that brings you joy and satisfaction.

GIVE YOURSELF AN AWARD for something you handled well today.

SKETCH YOUR FAVORITE PARTNER for snuggling. Is it a special blanket, a pet, or a loved one?

DRAW A FLOWER that fills you with happiness.

RECALL A TIME WHEN LOCKING EYES with someone brought you happiness.

_____

_____

_____

_____

_____

_____

PASTE A COPY OF YOUR FAVORITE COOKIE recipe below.
BONUS: Make the cookies this week, and share with a friend.

IMAGINE FIVE SENSATIONS on your face that make you smile.

1. _____

2. _____

3. _____

4. _____

5. _____

USE A BLANKET for something other than its intended purpose. Ideas: Set it on the floor or grass for a picnic, wear it as a cape, or play peek-a-boo with a baby. What did you choose?

RECALL THE BEST CONCERT you've ever attended. BONUS: Paste the ticket stub and photos below.

THINK OF A DETOUR in your life that turned out happier than the road you planned to take.

LIST FIVE WAYS you enjoy moving your body. **BONUS:** Choose one to do right now.

1. _____

2. _____

3. _____

4. _____

5. _____

CONGRATULATE YOURSELF for facing a fear this week—even if it was only Monday morning. What was the fear and how did you overcome it?

RECOGNIZE A TIME when swimming upstream paid off for your happiness or someone else's.

_____

_____

_____

_____

_____

_____

STAND AND STRETCH as tall as you can, imagining yourself as something that towers high into the sky. Draw what you imagined.

PROMISE YOURSELF A PAUSE. When can you allow yourself to do absolutely nothing without feeling a bit guilty about it?

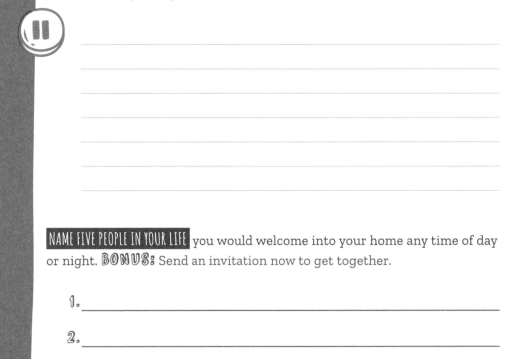

_____

_____

_____

_____

_____

_____

NAME FIVE PEOPLE IN YOUR LIFE you would welcome into your home any time of day or night. **BONUS:** Send an invitation now to get together.

1. _____

2. _____

3. _____

4. _____

5. _____

COME UP WITH YOUR COMIC BOOK or cartoon character catchphrase.

IDENTIFY THE PLACE you most enjoyed spending time today. What made it your happy place?

CREATE THE MOVIE MARATHON listing of your dreams. **BONUS:** Plan a time to make it happen.

_____   _____
_____   _____
_____   _____
_____   _____
_____   _____

CELEBRATE A CHANGE you made that may have seemed difficult at the time but has brought much happiness into your life.

_____
_____
_____
_____
_____

1. _____

2. _____

3. _____

4. _____

5. _____

REVISIT A COMPLIMENT that brought a huge smile to your face.

_____
_____
_____
_____
_____
_____
_____

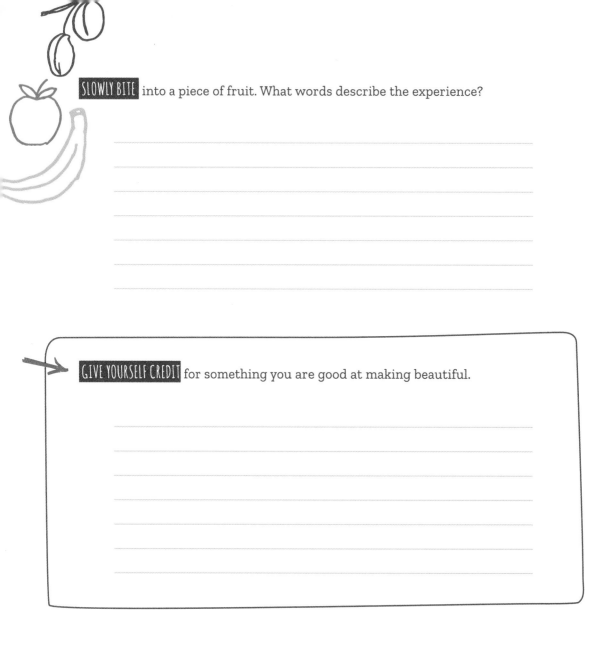

SLOWLY BITE into a piece of fruit. What words describe the experience?

GIVE YOURSELF CREDIT for something you are good at making beautiful.

THINK BACK TO THE LAST TIME you gave a standing ovation. What was the performance? Could you enjoy it again, or was it a once-in-a-lifetime experience?

_____

_____

_____

_____

_____

CELEBRATE FIVE JOYS unique to the age you are right now.

1. _____

2. _____

3. _____

4. _____

5. _____

WRITE A POSITIVE MESSAGE TO YOURSELF on your mirror with dry-erase marker. What did you write?

_____

_____

_____

_____

_____

WRITE A POSITIVE MESSAGE TO A LOVED ONE on a mirror with dry-erase marker. What did you write?

_____

_____

_____

_____

_____

_____

THINK OF A MOMENT your heart beat a little faster in a good way today.

_____

_____

_____

_____

_____

_____

_____

RECOGNIZE SOMETHING SILLY OR INDULGENT you do when no one is watching—maybe you dance around the house, make up songs, or lick the peanut butter jar.

_____

_____

_____

_____

_____

_____

TREAT YOURSELF TO A SCENT. Make coffee, bring in fresh flowers, or light a candle. What gift of scent will you give yourself?

_____
_____
_____
_____
_____
_____

CATCH SOMETHING—it could be a ball, soap bubbles, a train, or enthusiasm. What did you choose?

_____
_____
_____
_____
_____
_____

FILL IN THE BLANK with as many answers as come to mind: *I can't help but smile when* _____.

_____   _____
_____   _____
_____   _____
_____   _____
_____   _____
_____   _____

DRAW YOURSELF ON A MAGAZINE COVER. What would be the top positive headlines of your life so far?

DESCRIBE THE
BEST THING
you've ever won
and how it felt
to win.

MAKE AN ONLINE DONATION to a charity supporting work that's important to you.
What did you choose, and why?

SET A TIME to turn off the lights tonight—and honor it. Your mind and body deserve the pleasure of rest.

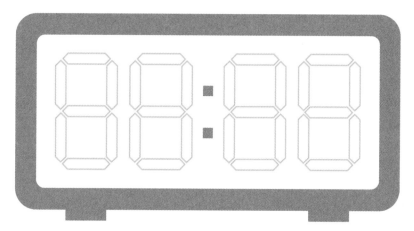

fill in the numbers

SHARE A TIME you've experienced contagious laughter.

PACK A BOOK IN YOUR BAG. Then brainstorm all the places you can treat yourself to a little reading on the go.

_____   _____
_____   _____
_____   _____
_____   _____
_____   _____

DESIGN A GINGERBREAD PERSON OR HOUSE. **BONUS:** Actually make it and share with loved ones.

LIST FIVE SHOWS that bring you happiness. **BONUS:** Plan to watch one this week.

1. _____

2. _____

3. _____

4. _____

5. _____

GRAB SOMETHING YOU CAN MANIPULATE with your hands—for example, modeling clay or a ball of yarn. Release the pressures of the day here and through your hands.

_____

_____

_____

_____

_____

_____

_____

MAKE A QUICK INTRODUCTION FOR YOURSELF. Is there someone you see regularly but you don't know his or her name? Plan to introduce yourself.

_____

_____

_____

_____

_____

_____

MAKE A QUICK INTRODUCTION FOR OTHERS. Whom can you bring together because you think they would be compatible personally or professionally?

_____

_____

_____

_____

_____

HELLO

MY NAME IS

CREATE AN ACROSTIC with your name. Write the letters of your name going down the page. Then use each letter to start a word that describes your best traits.

WATCH THE SUN RISE.

Commit to the time and place now. Then come back and describe how the experience made you feel.

_____

_____

_____

_____

RECALL THE MOST EXCITING SPORTING EVENT you've ever attended.

_____

_____

_____

_____

_____

_____

MAKE A LIST of goofy clubs you would love to start.

_____

_____

_____

_____

_____

_____

_____

WASH YOUR HANDS IN WARM WATER. What worries and regrets do you imagine going down the drain?

_____

_____

_____

_____

_____

LIST FIVE THINGS you consider sacred.

1. _____

2. _____

3. _____

4. _____

5. _____

WRITE ABOUT OR DRAW one sweet spot in your day.

DO A YOGA POSE. Then give it a new, secret name all your own, based on how it makes you feel.

_____

_____

_____

_____

_____

_____

NAME FIVE PLACES you always feel comfortable.

1. _____

2. _____

3. _____

4. _____

5. _____

CREATE A WINTER BUCKET LIST of activities you want to do before the season ends this year.

_____   _____
_____   _____
_____   _____
_____   _____
_____   _____
_____   _____

REACH OUT AND SHARE TOUCHES with loved ones. What opportunities are there to add more physical contact in your relationships?

_____
_____
_____
_____
_____
_____

CALL IN TO A RADIO STATION and make an old-fashioned request. What's the song and your dedication?

_____

_____

_____

_____

_____

_____

_____

MAKE A PLAN to add some houseplants or grow flowers, vegetables, fruit, or herbs. If you already have a host of plants, share one with a friend. What did you choose?

_____

_____

_____

_____

_____

_____

_____

DESIGN A BUMPER STICKER that makes you smile or laugh. **BONUS:** Have it printed.

CONNECT WITH AN OLD FRIEND on social media. What can you still laugh about?

LOOK UP THE HIGHEST ELEVATION in your area. Where is it, and when can you visit?

_____

_____

_____

_____

_____

RECITE A POSITIVE AFFIRMATION—even as simple as "I can." What will your happy words be? Write them in big, bold letters below.

WRITE ABOUT SOMETHING that makes you feel wild or unleashed.

PICK UP LITTER. Even small good deeds fill you with purpose, which leads to happiness. What area can you clean up? **BONUS:** Sponsor a cleanup group.

LEAVE A POSITIVE COMMENT on an online blog or article. How does it feel?

MAKE A TO-DO LIST for tomorrow.

Now go back and cross off at least three things.

DRAW WHAT YOU WANT your first glimpse of the day to be. Then make changes in your bedroom to position a certain piece of art, an inspirational quote, or the view out the window near your bed.

DO SOMETHING NICE for a neighbor—maybe pull trash cans back or set the newspaper at the end of the driveway closer to the house. How does it feel?

RECALL THE STRANGEST PLACE you've ever traveled.

_____

_____

_____

_____

_____

_____

DESCRIBE A FAVORITE FEATURE of, or a special item in, your living room.

_____

_____

_____

_____

_____

_____

_____

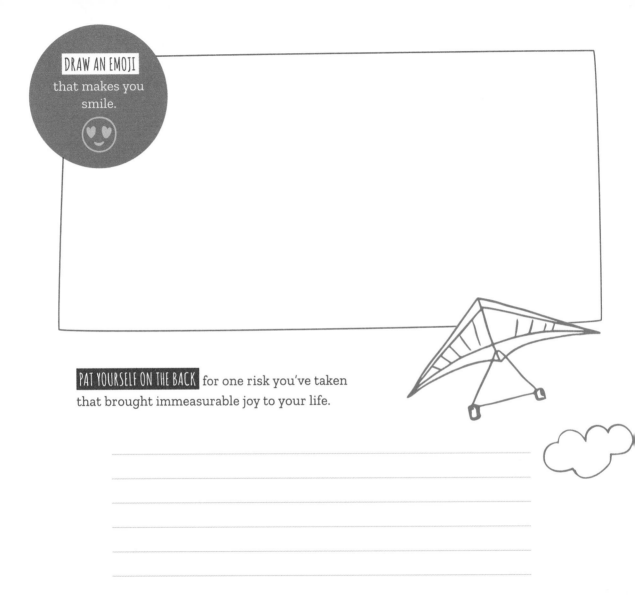

DRAW AN EMOJI that makes you smile.

PAT YOURSELF ON THE BACK for one risk you've taken that brought immeasurable joy to your life.

SEARCH FOR A GOOFY COMMERCIAL from your childhood. Is it as ridiculous as you remember? **BONUS:** Share it with a friend of similar age.

MARK THE PARTS of your body where you're ticklish.

THINK OF A TIME when you witnessed a happiness domino effect.

_____

_____

_____

_____

_____

_____

SCAN YOUR MIND BEFORE BED for any regrets you're holding on to. List them here, then flip your pillow over and promise to start fresh tomorrow.

_____

_____

_____

_____

_____

_____

1. _____
2. _____
3. _____
4. _____
5. _____

DESCRIBE A PIECE OF ARCHITECTURE that you find beautiful.

GRAB SOME CRAYONS or colored pencils, and draw anything that comes to mind. Set aside any judgment of artistic value.

CONSIDER THE BEST POSTCARD you ever received. Who sent it to you? Where did it come from? What did it say?

SHARE A GUARANTEED WAY to make your best friend smile.

_____

_____

_____

_____

_____

_____

_____

SHARE A GUARANTEED WAY to make your best friend laugh.

_____

_____

_____

_____

_____

_____

_____

IMAGINE YOU'RE CREATING a time capsule of your life right now. What would you include?

_____

_____

_____

_____

_____

_____

CELEBRATE FIVE THINGS IN NATURE that fill you with awe.

1. _____

2. _____

3. _____

4. _____

5. _____

COME UP WITH A REASON to have a party this week. **BONUS:** Actually throw a party.

DESCRIBE A TIME YOU FELT incredibly free.

REMEMBER THE LAST MEME that made you laugh out loud.

FILL IN THE BLANK with as many answers as come to mind: *I should be proud of myself for* _____.

LIST THE BEST THINGS TO ORDER at your favorite restaurant.
BONUS: Make a date to go there soon.

_____

_____

_____

_____

_____

SET YOUR ALARM to wake you up to a certain song. What song did you choose, and why?

_____

_____

_____

_____

_____

NAME A STORE that brings you happiness—even if just through browsing.
BONUS: Write the owner or manager a thank-you note for being part of your community and life.

SIMPLY DAYDREAM—give yourself permission to let your mind wander. When you come back, jot down any images or ideas you want to remember.

THINK BACK TO THE CRAZIEST thing you ever wanted to be when you grew up.

DRAW A GLASS that's half full. Then label what you'd like to drink in—literally or figuratively.

BUY ADVANCE TICKETS for a movie. What have you been wanting to see, and can now look forward to?

_____

_____

_____

_____

_____

_____

SAY A PRAYER or meditate on good wishes for someone you love. Record what went through your mind.

_____

_____

_____

_____

_____

_____

TELL A RUNNING INSIDE JOKE you have with a friend or family member.

_____

_____

_____

_____

_____

_____

PLAY IN THE DIRT—whether you plant something, pull a weed, or simply draw in the dirt with your finger. Beneficial, mood-boosting bacteria have been found in soil, plus it's just plain fun. Record your experience here.

_____

_____

_____

_____

_____

_____

THINK ABOUT ALL THE WAYS your body blesses you with what it allows you to do. Don't focus on any limitations, only the possibilities.

RECALL YOUR MOST MEMORABLE New Year's Eve.

BUY YOURSELF A BALLOON for no reason at all. Write or draw how it makes you feel.

RECORD THE BEST TRUTH someone has ever shared with you.

CREATE A GRATITUDE ALPHABET. Next to each letter, write the first thing that comes to mind when you think of what brings you happiness.

A _____

B _____

C _____

D _____

E _____

F _____

G _____

H _____

I _____

J _____

K _____

L _____

M _____

N _____

O _____

P _____

Q _____

R _____

S _____

T _____

U _____

V _____

W _____

X _____

Y _____

Z _____

DRAW A GAME PIECE from your favorite game.

WRITE A HAIKU about the best part of your week so far.

START AN ONLINE IDEA BOARD. Choose one goal in your life to focus on first.

_____

_____

_____

_____

_____

_____

LIST THE OUTDOOR SPACES —parks, forests, trails, beaches, and more—that have touched your life in a special way. **BONUS:** Visit one this week.

_____

_____

_____

_____

_____

SLOWLY BITE into a favorite dessert. What words describe the experience?

_____

_____

_____

_____

_____

_____

REMIND YOURSELF that you deserve to be happy. Sometimes that's all it takes to open your eyes and heart to happiness and new opportunities. Tell yourself and write it here in big letters: "I deserve to be happy."

IDENTIFY THE SILLIEST piece of clothing or accessory you own.
Use words and/or pictures.

LIST ALL THE THINGS YOU LOVE about your favorite museum.

FILL THIS PIÑATA with your favorite candies.

PLAN SOMEWHERE NEW you can go this week—even if it's just a different coffee shop, post office, or gas station.

_____

_____

_____

_____

_____

_____

_____

GIVE SOMEONE A COMPLIMENT. What was the reaction?

_____

_____

_____

_____

_____

_____

_____

1. _____

2. _____

3. _____

4. _____

5. _____

FRESHEN UP THE HOME SCREEN of your phone with a new photo that brings you joy. What did you choose?

RECALL A TIME you were able to come to someone else's rescue—physically or emotionally.

_____

_____

_____

_____

_____

_____

_____

WEAR A BRIGHT COLOR. What did you choose, and how did it make you feel?

_____

_____

_____

_____

_____

DESCRIBE YOUR LAST BIKE RIDE. **BONUS:** Ride a bike this week.

_____

_____

_____

_____

_____

_____

THINK OF TWO OF YOUR FAVORITE animals. Then draw a mashup of them below.

SIGN UP FOR A CHARITY WALK or run. What cause will you be supporting?

DRAW YOURSELF CROSSING the finish line of the above event.

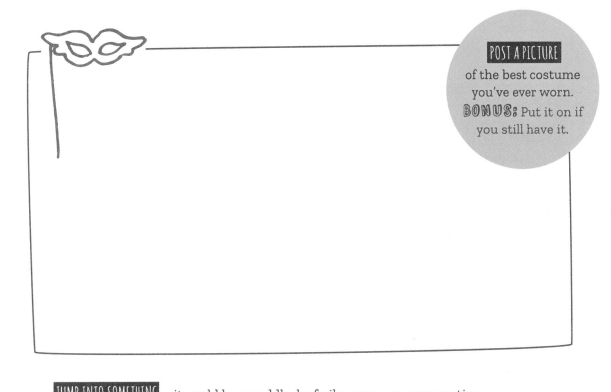

POST A PICTURE of the best costume you've ever worn. **BONUS:** Put it on if you still have it.

JUMP INTO SOMETHING—it could be a puddle, leaf pile, game, or conversation. What did you choose?

_____

_____

_____

_____

_____

CONFESS TO THREE STRANGE COMBINATIONS that bring you happiness.

_____ + _____

_____ + _____

_____ + _____

SEND A FRIEND A GOOFY GIF. What was the reaction?

_____

_____

_____

_____

_____

_____

_____

CREATE YOUR OWN MAGICAL SPELL that will make you smile when you need it, even if it doesn't truly work magic in a literal sense.

THINK BACK TO A TIME when finding something lost brought you joy.

_____

_____

_____

_____

_____

_____

#1

LIST ALL THE THINGS YOU LOVE about your favorite sport.
BONUS: Play the sport or watch an event.

_____   _____
_____   _____
_____   _____
_____   _____
_____   _____
_____   _____

WRAP A GIFT. What's inside, and who is the recipient?

_____
_____
_____
_____
_____
_____
_____

CELEBRATE SMALL TASKS. Made a phone call you've been putting off? Finished a project at home or work? Give yourself space in that moment to simply recognize what you accomplished and do nothing more. Where might you be able to find these types of reasons to celebrate this week?

SET A TARGET DATE for a reunion. Family or friends? What are you most looking forward to?

TOSS OUT SOMETHING long overdue from your kitchen. How does accomplishing this simple task make you feel?

 **SKETCH A PATTERN** that makes you happy.

CREATE A SUMMER BUCKET LIST of activities you want to do before the season ends this year.

_____   _____
_____   _____
_____   _____
_____   _____
_____   _____
_____   _____

POST A FAVORITE MOVIE LINE on social media. Who instantly gets the reference?

_____
_____
_____
_____
_____
_____

RANK THE THREE BEST CLASSES you've ever taken.

1. _____
_____

2. _____
_____

3. _____
_____

LIST THREE THINGS you could teach a class about—don't worry if they're a little crazy.

1. _____
_____

2. _____
_____

3. _____
_____

THINK ABOUT A VOICE you could listen to for hours. What about it makes you happy?

_____

_____

_____

_____

_____

CREATE YOUR PERFECT PIZZA below. Thin or thick crust? What are your toppings?
BONUS: Put it on the menu for a lunch or dinner this week.

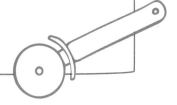

CHOOSE YOUR FAVORITE DAY of the year. Think about why you love it so much.

CELEBRATE A GIFT OF HEALTH you were given after a time of not feeling well. What helped you heal?

MAKE A TOAST. Don't wait for a special occasion or champagne. You can toast a friend or coworker over coffee. Whom will you toast, and what will you say?

_____
_____
_____
_____
_____

PLAY A SONG that makes you want to dance, then do just that with abandon. How does it feel?

_____
_____
_____
_____
_____
_____
_____

RECALL SOMETHING you were pleased to have been able to fix—from an appliance to a relationship.

_____

_____

_____

_____

_____

SEND SOMEONE A BOUQUET of flowers anonymously. Who is the recipient, and what encouraging message accompanies the gift?

_____

_____

_____

_____

_____

DRAW YOUR FAVORITE WAY to get from point A to point B.

CREATE A LIST OF TRAITS you're grateful you've received from family members. **BONUS:** Share it with your family.

_____	_____
_____	_____
_____	_____
_____	_____
_____	_____
_____	_____

TAKE THREE DEEP BREATHS. On each exhale, release a situation or factor that's holding you back from happiness. Release them here as well.

1. _____
   _____

2. _____
   _____

3. _____
   _____

WRITE INSTRUCTIONS to a child on how to find happiness.
BONUS: Share it with a child in your life.

1. _____

2. _____

3. _____

4. _____

5. _____

SIT UP STRAIGHT. Straighter posture can actually boost confidence, energy, and mood.
Where do you find yourself slumping the most that you can watch for?

_____

_____

_____

_____

_____

_____

_____

CONSIDER AN OPPORTUNITY that may come out of a setback you've recently experienced.

DRAW AN ICE CREAM SUNDAE or a cupcake with all the extras. Studies show that drawing pictures of junk foods can provide the same sense of satisfaction as eating them.

JOT DOWN 10 THINGS with the first 10 sips of your morning coffee, tea, or juice that you're looking forward to in the next week.

1. _____

2. _____

3. _____

4. _____

5. _____

6. _____

7. _____

8. _____

9. _____

10. _____

BLOW OUT A CANDLE, and make a wish. Record it below. Don't reserve the fun for birthdays!

_____

_____

_____

_____

_____

_____

SAY THANK YOU. Jot down a few people who deserve your thanks and the reasons why. **BONUS:** Follow through with that thanks.

_____ *because* _____

_____

_____ *because* _____

_____

_____ *because* _____

_____

WRITE A GLOWING ONLINE REVIEW for a business or provider from which you received great service. Plan what you'll say here.

_____

_____

_____

_____

⭐ ⭐ ⭐ ⭐ ⭐

BREAK FOR LEMONADE OR PRODUCE. The next time you see a roadside stand, stop and support the kids or farmers. How does it make you feel?

_____

_____

_____

_____

_____

COME UP WITH A PHRASE to remind yourself that bad days pass.

ADD A PLEASING SCENT to your car. What did you choose and why?

IMAGINE YOURSELF feeling happy. What people, sights, smells, and sounds surround you?

SEARCH FOR A VIDEO that starts with the title, "cute baby [fill in the blank with an animal or action]." What did you find to make you smile? **BONUS:** Share it with a friend.

MASSAGE SOME LOTION into your hands. As you rub in circles, choose words of positivity to sink in as well.

LEARN A NEW WORD —in your first language or a new language. Write your word and its meaning below.

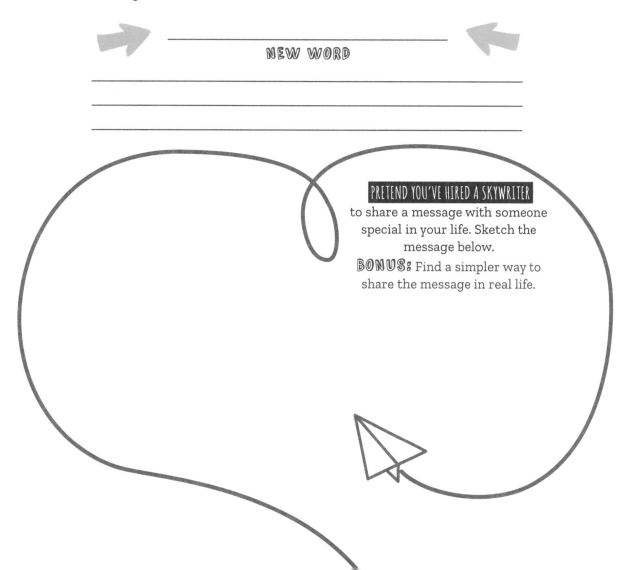

NEW WORD

PRETEND YOU'VE HIRED A SKYWRITER to share a message with someone special in your life. Sketch the message below.
BONUS: Find a simpler way to share the message in real life.

BREAK OUT IN A SKIP sometime during your day. How does it feel?

SIT QUIETLY AND LISTEN. Write down all the sounds you can hear that communicate energy and life.

THINK ABOUT WHAT DOTS have connected in your life in a surprisingly pleasant way. Illustrate the connections here.

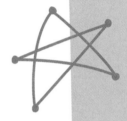

TAKE A PHOTO of the first thing that makes you smile as you go about your day—no matter how ordinary it is. Come back and paste it here.

MAKE A LIST of all the "faults" you love about someone close to you.
BONUS: Share it with that person.

- ○ _____
- ○ _____
- ○ _____
- ○ _____
- ○ _____
- ○ _____

MAKE A LIST of all the imperfections in yourself that you've come to accept.

- ○ _____
- ○ _____
- ○ _____
- ○ _____
- ○ _____
- ○ _____

LIST THE ADDRESSES of the last three places you've lived, plus what you loved most about living there.

1. _____
_____
_____
_____

2. _____
_____
_____
_____

3. _____
_____
_____
_____

IMAGINE HOW SOMEONE would describe the most beautiful parts of you and your life.

RECALL THE BEST SURPRISE you ever received.

MARVEL AT THE SMALLEST THINGS
you've seen in nature.

_____

_____

_____

_____

_____

_____

_____

_____

MARVEL AT THE BIGGEST THINGS
you've seen in nature.

_____

_____

_____

_____

_____

_____

_____

_____

LOOK FOR A JOYFUL IMAGE in the clouds. Draw what you find here.

REMIND YOURSELF of three things you were smart and strong to walk away from and leave in the past in exchange for your present happiness.

1. _____

2. _____

3. _____

CHANGE A SOCIAL MEDIA PROFILE name to something goofy for one day. Does anyone notice?

_____

_____

_____

_____

_____

GIVE YOURSELF CREDIT for part-of-the-way victories. In what areas have you made progress even if you haven't reached the ultimate goals?

_____

_____

_____

_____

_____

_____

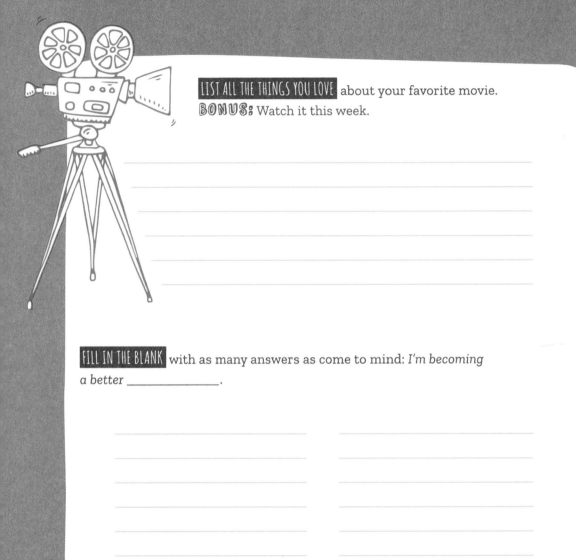

LIST ALL THE THINGS YOU LOVE about your favorite movie.
BONUS: Watch it this week.

FILL IN THE BLANK with as many answers as come to mind: *I'm becoming a better* _____.

LOOK AHEAD TO THREE EVENTS or experiences in the next month that you're excited about.

1. _____

2. _____

3. _____

CHOOSE A PERSON who somehow grabs your attention in the course of your day. In your head, wish them a day filled with good things. What went through your mind, and how did you feel?

THINK OF AN OBJECT that makes you smile. Then place it by the entrance of your home, so that it's the first sight you see each time you return. What did you choose?

DESCRIBE IN WORDS OR PICTURES what your body feels like when you're happy.

DESCRIBE IN WORDS OR PICTURES what your mind feels like when you're happy.

RECALL AT LEAST ONE TIME when a complete stranger helped you.

_____

_____

_____

_____

_____

_____

_____

RECORD AT LEAST ONE WAY (big or small) you helped a complete stranger this week.

_____

_____

_____

_____

_____

_____

_____

CREATE A SPRING BUCKET LIST of activities you want to do before the season ends this year.

ATTACH A PHOTO OF, OR DRAW, A VIEW that you appreciate in your day-to-day travels.

REMEMBER A TIME a long search or wait in your life had a happy ending.

_____

_____

_____

_____

_____

_____

_____

RUN AFTER SOMETHING —it could be your dog, an ice-cream truck, a person who's left an item behind, or an opportunity. What did you choose?

_____

_____

_____

_____

_____

_____

1. _____

2. _____

3. _____

4. _____

5. _____

ASK FOR HELP with a task or responsibility that's leaving you feeling burdened. Whom can you enlist for support?

_____

_____

_____

_____

_____

_____

_____

GIVE THANKS for the jobs you've held that have taught you important lessons. **BONUS:** Reach out to your managers and/or coworkers from those jobs.

_____

_____

_____

_____

_____

_____

GIVE THANKS for the family roles you've held that have brought you blessings.

_____

_____

_____

_____

_____

_____

SKETCH YOURSELF AS A SUPERHERO with everyday powers emanating from you for which you can feel gratitude. Remember that seemingly simple traits, such as kindness, are still very powerful.

RECOGNIZE GROUPS

and communities who lift your spirit.

APPRECIATE YOUR QUIRKS and silly talents that make others laugh.
BONUS: Laugh at yourself.

LOOK BACK to a shut door in your life that opened up an even better opportunity. What happened, and what was the outcome?

_____

_____

_____

_____

_____

IDENTIFY YOUR FAVORITE TIME of the week. How can you preserve this time? Are there ways to bring elements of this time into other parts of your week, or is the unique time what makes it special?

_____

_____

_____

_____

_____

_____

THINK OF THE CHILDREN in your life who bring you happiness. **BONUS:** Attach a photo.

DESCRIBE THE MOST BEAUTIFUL wedding you ever attended.

REACH OUT AND TOUCH something that brings you calm and happiness—maybe a favorite fluffy blanket or the soft fur of a dog or cat's head. What touches hold the most power for you?

_____

_____

_____

_____

_____

STACK YOUR HAPPINESS DECK by first venting the negatives of your day, but then recognizing twice as many positives.

NEGATIVE	POSITIVE

COME UP WITH AS MANY SONGS as you can in a minute that make you feel happy.
BONUS: Create a playlist.

LOOK AT SOMETHING in nature as if seeing it for the first time. Describe it in words and sketches below.

BRIGHTEN UP with more light. Wherever you are spending time, look for a window, switch on a soft lamp, light a candle, or illuminate with string lights. How does light affect your mood?

LIST THE NUMBERS or names that make you smile when they pop up on your phone. **BONUS:** Assign specific ringtones to these contacts, if you haven't already.

ADD SOMETHING TO YOUR BAG or wallet that will make you smile when you see it throughout the day. What did you choose?

_____

_____

_____

_____

_____

ADD SOMETHING TO A LOVED ONE'S BAG or wallet that will make him or her smile when it's found. What did you choose?

_____

_____

_____

_____

_____

_____

MAKE SOMETHING OUT OF PAPER—an airplane, a football, or a snowflake perhaps. Describe in words or pictures what you created.

FILL THIS SPACE with as many words as you can that you associate with happiness. **BONUS:** Make a copy and frame it to place somewhere it will inspire you.

OUTLINE THE RULES of a game or sport you invented with friends or family.

RECORD A SMALL SURPRISE that made your day brighter.

POUR YOURSELF A CUP of tea or coffee. As you pour, imagine these good vibes and feelings filling your cup—and your day.

_____   _____
_____   _____
_____   _____
_____
_____
_____

DESCRIBE A FAVORITE FEATURE of, or a special item in, your dining area.

_____
_____
_____
_____
_____
_____
_____

LIST FIVE PURPLE THINGS that make you happy.

1. _____

2. _____

3. _____

4. _____

5. _____

RECALL SOMETHING KIND you did for yourself.

_____
_____
_____
_____
_____
_____
_____

WRITE DOWN, OR DRAW A MAP to the location of the nearest swing set. Then make a plan to sneak in some swinging.

FILL THIS SPACE with everything you love about your family.

BONUS: Share some of the thoughts with family members.

 PEEK BACK at any random page of this journal whenever you need a boost of happiness!